NATURAL WORLD

LEOPARD

HABITATS • LIFE CYCLES • FOOD CHAINS • THREATS

Bill Jordan

Wayland

an imprint of Hodder
Children's Books

WWF

Produced in Association with WWF-UK

NATURAL WORLD

Chimpanzee • Crocodile • Black Rhino • Dolphin • Elephant
Giant Panda • Giraffe • Golden Eagle • Great White Shark
Grizzly Bear • Hippopotamus • Killer Whale • Leopard • Lion
Orangutan • Penguin • Polar Bear • Tiger

Produced for Hodder Wayland by
Roger Coote Publishing
Gissing's Farm, Fressingfield
Suffolk IP21 5SH, UK

WWF is a registered charity no. 1081247
WWF-UK, Panda House, Weyside Park
Godalming, Surrey GU7 1XR

Cover: A snarling leopard, up close.

Title page: A young leopard rests on a tree branch.

Contents page: A leopard looks for prey from a rock.

Index page: A leopard relaxes in a tree, safe from lions and hyenas.

Editor: Polly Goodman
Series editor: Victoria Brooker
Designer: Victoria Webb

Published in Great Britain in 2001 by Hodder Wayland,
an imprint of Hodder Children's Books

First published in paperback in 2001

British Library Cataloguing in Publication Data
Jordan, Bill, 1924-
Leopard. - (Natural World)
1.Leopard- Juvenile literature
I.Title
599.7'554

ISBN 0 7502 3413 X

Printed and bound by G. Canale & C.S.p.A., Turin, Italy

Hodder Children's Books
A division of Hodder Headline Limited
338 Euston Road, London NW1 3BH

Picture acknowledgements
Ardea 9 John Daniels, 11, 17, 25, 39, 44 (middle)
Ferrero-Labat, 20, 44 (bottom) M. Watson, 28 Francois
Gohier, 33 S. Meyers, 37 C. Clem Haagner, 41 Nick
Gordon; *Bruce Coleman Collection* 8 Erwin & Peggy
Bauer, 10, 44 (top) Alain Compost, 12, 30, 36 Kim
Taylor; *Corbis* 29, 38 Tom Brakefield, 31 William Doe,
35, 45 (middle) Anthony Bannister, 40 Buddy Mays;
Digital Vision 1, 3, 6, 19, 45 (bottom), 48; *Getty Images* 7
Renee Lynn; *Natural Visions* Cover Heather Angel;
NHPA 13 Peter Pickford, 16 Kevin Schafer, 18, 27 Nigel
Dennis, 15, 22 Martin Harvey, 23 A. Warburton & S.
Toon, 24, 34 Andy Rouse, 32, 45 (top) Stephen
Krasemann; *Oxford Scientific Films* 21 F. Polking; *Still
Pictures* 14, 42 Martin Wendler, 43 Mathieu Labourer;
Artwork by Michael Posen.

Contents

Meet the Leopard

The leopard is a large, graceful cat. It is the most widespread member of the cat family and the third-largest member. Only the lion and the tiger are bigger. It lives in Africa, south of the Sahara desert, and in Asia.

Neck
The leopard's powerful neck muscles allow it to carry three times its own body weight high up into the trees.

Ears
Leopards have exceptionally good hearing, which is better than a tiger's.

Eyes
Leopards have enormous, greenish-yellow eyes. At night they dilate so much that the leopard can see in the dark.

Nose
Leopards have an excellent sense of smell.

Teeth
A leopard has very strong teeth, perfectly shaped for killing prey and tearing flesh from the bone.

Claws
The leopard's sharp claws retract when they are not being used. They are used to tear into the flesh of prey and help climb trees.

4

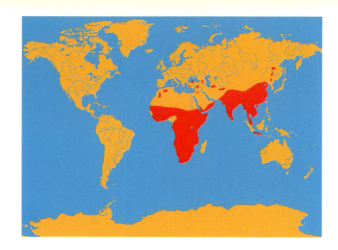

▲ The red shading on this map shows where leopards live.

▼ An adult leopard.

LEOPARD FACTS

The leopard's scientific name is *Panthera pardus*.

●

The name 'leopard' comes from the Greek words for lion (*leo*) and panther (*pardos*), which it was once thought to be.

●

Leopards measure up to 70 centimetres tall at the shoulder and 230 centimetres long from head to tail.

●

Males weigh up to 90 kilograms and females weigh up to 60 kilograms.

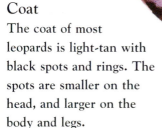

Coat
The coat of most leopards is light-tan with black spots and rings. The spots are smaller on the head, and larger on the body and legs.

Tail
A leopard's tail can be up to 90 centimetres long. It has dark rings and a black tip.

Legs
The leopard uses its strong legs to run at speeds of 60 kilometres an hour. It can leap over a distance of 6 metres and jump 3 metres high.

Hunting and habitat

Leopards are fast runners. They are also good at leaping, climbing trees and even swimming, so they are excellent hunters.

Leopards live in grasslands, woodlands and riverside forests. They can survive in any habitat where there is thick vegetation, but woodlands and open forests are favourites. There they can sit safely in the branches of trees, looking out for prey.

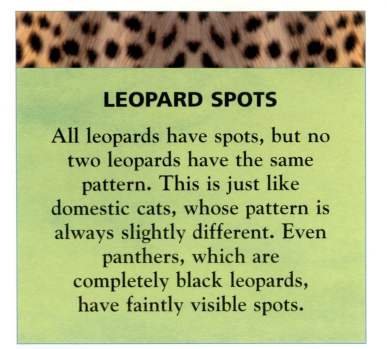

LEOPARD SPOTS

All leopards have spots, but no two leopards have the same pattern. This is just like domestic cats, whose pattern is always slightly different. Even panthers, which are completely black leopards, have faintly visible spots.

▼ Strolling through the grassland, a leopard is well-camouflaged by its coat.

▲ Black leopards are also known as panthers. They are found most often on the Malay peninsula.

The leopard's coat provides excellent camouflage in the dappled sunlight of the forests. It also helps the leopard hide in dense thickets out in the grasslands. Even when it crouches in more open grassland, the leopard is almost impossible to see. Only movement can give its presence away.

The leopard shares its range with many different animals. Some, such as gazelle, bush pigs and wart hogs are its prey. Others, such as lions, hyenas, cheetahs and jackals are competitors for food.

7

Relatives

The leopard is a member of the cat family, which includes thirty-seven species. Cats are divided into big cats and small cats. The big cat family includes the leopard, tiger, lion, jaguar, snow leopard, clouded leopard and cheetah.

Within the leopard family there are seven sub-species, depending on where they live in the world. The North African leopard, which is featured in this book, is the most numerous, but even this leopard is threatened.

▼ A clouded leopard in Southeast Asia.

CLOUDED AND SNOW LEOPARDS

The clouded leopard and the snow leopard are closely related to true leopards, but they are actually separate species. The snow leopard lives in the high mountains of Central Asia. It has long, whitish fur. The clouded leopard lives in the forests of Southeast Asia. Like the true leopard, it has a yellowish coat marked with spots and stripes. Both clouded and snow leopards are endangered species.

▲ The snow leopard's light-coloured fur is good camouflage in its snowy habitat.

The other six sub-species are extremely rare and some may already be extinct. They include the Amur leopard, which lives in North China and Korea. There are said to be only forty Amur leopards left in the wild. Other leopards include the Anatolian leopard of Asia, the Barbary and South Arabian leopards of the Middle East, and the Zanzibar leopard, which may be extinct.

A Leopard is Born

As she nears the time to give birth, a heavily pregnant female leopard looks for a safe den to have her family. This is usually a cave, a rock crevice or a dense thicket, where she will be hidden from other animals. The cubs have been growing inside her for about three and a half months.

At birth, the cubs have dark, woolly fur. Within minutes they find their mother's teats and drink her milk. The mother is very protective and attentive in these early days. She suckles, cleans and keeps her cubs warm, and for the first few days, she won't leave them at all. She knows that they could be taken by lions, hyenas or even eagles. If there is any threatening danger, the mother may move them from the den to a safer place.

▼ These leopard cubs are just ten days old.

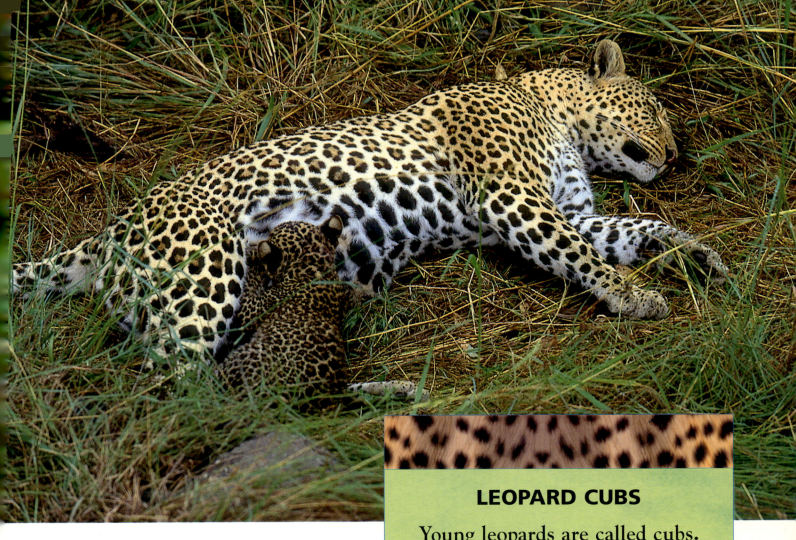

▲ A two-month-old cub drinking its mother's milk in Kenya.

At birth the cubs' eyes are tightly shut, but they can hear. Their eyes open at about seven to ten days and they can walk within ten days.

The cubs will remain hidden in the den until they are about eight weeks old. Since their mother doesn't make a bed for them, the cubs have to lie on the ground or on bare rock.

LEOPARD CUBS

Young leopards are called cubs. A new-born cub may be 15 centimetres tall and weigh $1/2$ kilogram.

●

Female leopards usually have between one and three cubs in the wild, but they can have up to six. The mother would have difficulty in rearing more than two cubs in the wild. She may have enough milk, but catching enough prey to feed them as they grew up would be hard.

Early days

The cubs grow rapidly in their first few weeks. By the time they are one month old they have doubled their weight at birth. At this age, the mother begins to bring back part of the prey she has killed and tears off small pieces of meat to give to her cubs. To begin with the cubs are not fussy about the food she brings, but soon they eat ravenously.

▼ A mother leopard and her cub rubbing noses. Mothers are very affectionate towards their cubs.

GROWTH RATE

At birth, a cub weighs $^1/_2$ kilogram. At six months it weighs 10 kilograms, at twelve months it weighs 30 kilograms and at two years it weighs 60 kilograms.

▲ A young leopard cub peers out at the world from the cover of bushes.

Cubs are very playful. They are particularly attracted to the black tip of their mother's tail, which they try to pounce on. When their mother returns from hunting there is a great demonstration of affection. She purrs like a domestic cat.

However, when the mother suspects danger she will hiss. This is a sign to the cubs to freeze, or stand absolutely still. Freezing is an instinctive reaction that many animals do to help them survive. The eyes of enemies find it easier to see movement, so by keeping absolutely still it is easier to remain unnoticed.

Cubs at risk

Gradually, meat becomes a greater part of the cubs' diet as their mother's milk dries up. At the age of three months they are weaned. To provide her cubs with enough food, the mother has to spend much more time hunting. This means she has to leave her cubs for longer periods, not only at night but also during the day.

▲ A leopardess stands beside her dead cub in Kenya.

This is one of the most vulnerable times of the young cubs' lives. If they don't remain hidden, predators can find them easily. In the daylight, the cubs become restless and may give away their presence. Eagles have excellent eyesight and can spot a small cub from high up in the sky. They can quickly swoop down and grab a surprised cub between their talons. Baboons, which are frightened of adult leopards, will not hesitate to swing down from the trees to kill an unprotected cub. Lions and hyenas are always on the look-out for easy pickings.

The mother cannot protect her cubs all the time because leopards are solitary animals. Unlike lions, who live in prides, leopards live alone. The male leopard takes no part in rearing the family, so the cubs have no protection from their father.

▼ This young leopard has been killed by lions.

15

Learning to Survive

In their first two years, the cubs are taught how to survive in the wild. First, they are taught to kill for food. Their mother brings them a small live animal, such as a cane rat or a bird, and allows them to kill it. If the animal tries to escape, the cubs chase and catch it. They begin to learn about basic hunting skills.

Next the cubs learn how to climb trees. Their mother climbs a little way up a tree and encourages the cubs to follow. Their sharp claws make this easy at first, but it is much more difficult coming down. At first they try to come down head-first, but their claws are pointing the wrong way and they often tumble to the ground. Soon they learn to descend tail-first, digging their claws into the tree-trunk to stop them slipping.

▶ Seven-month-old cubs learning how to climb trees. Leopard cubs seem to have no fear of heights. They will happily run along the branch of a tree, high above the ground.

▼ A leopardess with a hare she has caught. If it is alive, it could be good practice for the cubs to chase and catch.

Scent-marking

Another important lesson for the cubs is learning about territories and scent-marking. The mother will take her cubs to trees, shrubs or rocks that she has scent-marked by spraying them with her urine. The urine contains a scent that only belongs to the mother. No two scent-marks are the same. From the smell of a scent-mark, other leopards can tell whether it has been made by a male or a female, and whether or not the female is on heat.

▲ This leopard is scent-marking its territory in Kruger National Park, South Africa.

The cubs may begin to spray on the same spot as their mother. As they get older she may take them to the edge of her territory, where there may be marks made by another leopard. They learn that they should not cross into that region.

Once the cubs are strong enough to climb trees easily, the family leaves the den where the cubs were born. The cubs begin to meet other animals that share their habitat. They learn to avoid snakes and porcupines, which they are tempted to try and catch. Porcupine quills are sharp and wounds from the quills can become infected.

◀ Poisonous snakes like this cobra can give a cub a deadly bite if they tread on one by accident.

19

Hunting

During the day, the mother will take her older cubs hunting, to show them how to use their camouflage. She will teach them how to creep slowly and stealthily towards prey animals, and how to patiently remain still if the animals look towards them. Now and again the cubs may flush out a ground bird or small animal, which the mother can catch.

At night, their mother hunts alone. This is the most important hunting time for leopards. Their eyesight is particularly good for seeing in the dark.

◀ Tall grass hides a mother and her cub well as she takes it out on a hunting lesson.

▶ An adult leopard searches for prey in the Masai Mara Game Reserve, in Kenya.

Hearing

It is their acute hearing that helps leopards hunt the most. Leopards can hear the slightest rustle of leaves or grass several metres away and will immediately freeze and stand motionless, listening and waiting to hear the sound again. They may even be able to tell what the animal is from the sound of its footsteps. The quick, repeated steps of a small animal are different from the regular, quiet tread of a larger animal.

▼ A leopard crouches low in the grass as it stalks its prey.

▲ A male leopard gets ready to pounce on its prey in Namibia.

The leopard may edge closer, placing its paws slowly and carefully so it does not make a noise. The whole time it is listening for any change in sounds. It may even leap upon the animal before it actually sees it.

Smell

Leopards also use their excellent sense of smell to help them hunt. They can tell what an animal is from its scent, and they can also tell if the scent is old or new.

23

The kill

The Kiswahili people in Africa call the leopard *chui*, which means 'one that kills with a single leap'. However, before it makes a kill, the leopard stealthily stalks its prey to get as close as possible. Leopards catch most of their prey by the throat and kill it by squeezing hard on its blood vessels. This cuts off the blood supply to the brain, which causes immediate unconsciousness and rapid death. Smaller prey may be killed with a single bite to the back of the neck. The bite breaks the prey's neck, killing it instantly.

▼ Leopards can chase their prey at speeds of up to 60 kilometres an hour.

24

▶ This leopard has caught a Thompson's gazelle and is feeding on it in a tree-top. Leopards can easily drag animals weighing 70 kilograms up into a tree. They have even been known to carry young giraffes.

After the kill, the leopard will usually carry its prey high up into a tree to prevent losing it to a lion or hyena. High up in the tree-tops, the leopard can dine off the carcass for several days in comfort.

If the prey is too big to drag up a tree, there is a good chance that a lion or hyena will smell the blood and drive the leopard away before it can have a good feed.

LEOPARD FOOD CHAIN

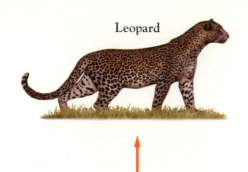

Leopard

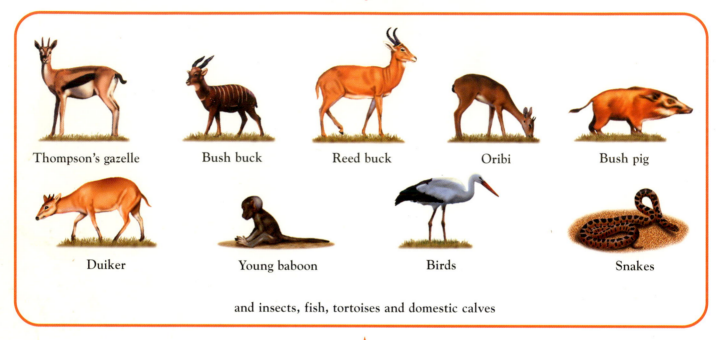

Thompson's gazelle   Bush buck   Reed buck   Oribi   Bush pig

Duiker   Young baboon   Birds   Snakes

and insects, fish, tortoises and domestic calves

Leaves, fruits, seeds, bulbs, roots and grasses

▲ The leopard feeds on almost thirty different species, from young giraffes to dung beetles. The wide range of its diet helps make it the most successful hunter of the cat family.

Diet

A leopard's diet depends on where it lives. In the open grasslands of Africa, it will hunt and eat big prey such as Thompson's gazelle, which weighs about 20 kilograms, or impala. Occasionally it may tackle a 200-kilogram wildebeest if it looks old and weak, or injured.

Leopards also prey on smaller animals, including bush pigs, duiker, birds of different kinds and even catfish.

▼ A bush pig foraging for bulbs and tubers to eat.

Avoiding injury

The leopard is the strongest big cat of its size. Its teeth are stronger than a lion's and if cornered, it can inflict terrible injuries on its enemies. However, since it is a solitary animal and cannot rely on food from other leopards, as lions can in a pride, a leopard will avoid any injury that might reduce its ability to hunt. So whenever possible, leopards will hurry away from danger rather than confront it.

▲ A leopard's strong canine teeth tear into the flesh of its prey.

Leopards and baboons hate each other. Baboons will kill leopard cubs if they can and they can ruin a leopard's hunting tactics. When they see a leopard from the tree-tops, baboons screech and shout. This alarm call alerts all the other animals nearby, which means the leopard is unable to hunt.

Out on open ground, single baboons are easy prey for a leopard to kill and eat because baboons cannot run as fast as leopards. But among the trees, large male baboons will rush to the rescue, moving swiftly through the tree-tops. The leopard will turn and run because it knows that although it can easily kill one baboon, it cannot fight several at once.

▶ This baboon is just out of the leopard's reach on the outer branches of a tree.

Prey from farms

When new farms are built on a leopard's territory they can drive away its prey. The leopard may start preying on farm animals and dogs instead. However, leopards are cautious about humans, so they are rarely seen.

Some farmers don't mind having a leopard on their land, even though it may kill a calf from time to time, because they know that a leopard will keep baboons away. Baboons can enter and destroy a field of crops. Even if dogs drive them off, they will return as soon as the dogs are gone.

But the smell of a leopard will keep baboons away. They know that it is so stealthy and well-camouflaged that it could surprise and kill them before they could run to the safety of trees.

Although the leopard rarely attacks people, it is very dangerous when approached and will kill people if it feels threatened. It can be terrifying when angry.

▶ A leopard can leap over a distance of 6 metres.

▼ Troops of baboons are often on the ground. They can feed on fields of crops.

Adult Life

Between two and three years old, the cubs become fully grown adults. It is time to leave their mother and find their own territory. This is a difficult task. The mother may share her territory with her female young for a while, but they must keep out of their mother's way.

Young leopards may have to travel a long way to find their own territory, keeping out of the way of other leopards whose territories they pass through. If they are lucky, they will find an empty region where a leopard has died, or where there is an old, weak leopard they can drive out.

▲ It would be easy to miss this leopard in the tall grass of the Serengeti Plains, in Kenya.

TERRITORIES

Territories change size depending on the amount of prey animals available. If there are lots of prey animals, leopards do not need very large territories. However, if there are few prey animals, each leopard will need a bigger area of land to hunt for food.

●

Female territories are about 12 to 40 square kilometres, depending on food supply. Male territories are larger and may overlap with those belonging to females.

●

Leopards can travel 25 kilometres over their territory in one night, or up to 75 kilometres if they are disturbed.

The young leopards begin to make scent-marks, which will make any resident leopard angry. There may be fights as the young leopards try to find their own territories.

Leopards are always on the move within their own territories, but they don't migrate like lions. Even though some of their favourite prey species move away, there are always some animals or birds left to hunt. Leopards' territories are large and the chances of meeting another leopard by accident are slim.

▶ Play-fighting helps young leopards develop muscles and agility for survival when they are fully grown.

Ready to mate

There is no particular breeding season for leopards, so they mate at any time of the year. A female leopard will come on heat after her cubs have left.

When a female comes on heat, her scent-marks contain a particular smell, which is carried many miles by the breeze. It is a clear signal to the nearest male, who will travel a long way to mate with the female.

If more than one male arrives, they will fight over the female until one retreats. Fights between rival leopards may look savage, but they try not to get badly injured. It is certainly not a fight to the death.

▲ This leopard is snarling aggressively.

BREEDING

A female leopard is ready to mate when she reaches two years old. She will come on heat every three to seven weeks until she becomes pregnant, and she will be on heat for two or three days each time. A female leopard will give birth every two years.

▶ Two leopards prepare to mate.

Mating is very quick and is repeated many times. After mating, the male leopard will stay with the female until she is pregnant, before returning to his own territory. The cubs will never know their father.

Females can mate before they have established a territory of their own. If prey is scarce and the female is inexperienced at hunting, she will not be able to feed her cubs.

A leopard's day

Since leopards hunt mainly at night, a typical day in the life of a leopard is quite lazy. Resting in the day saves energy for a night of activity.

Leopards usually doze on a large branch in a tree, safe from lions and hyenas. Here they can enjoy the breeze in the heat of the day while keeping their ears alert for any passing prey.

▲ A full and content leopard dozes beside the remains of its meal. The carcass is from a springbok, a type of antelope.

Another favourite resting place in the late afternoon is on a rocky outcrop, which will be comfortably warm. The leopard keeps itself clean and licks small wounds caused by thorns or sharp stones. Its saliva, like that of many carnivores including the domestic dog, stimulates healing and helps to prevent infection.

If it hears the slightest sound, the leopard will raise its head and carefully climb down from the tree or rocks without making a sound. Creeping towards the direction of the sound, the leopard may be lucky enough to catch a midday snack.

If the leopard is hungry, it will prowl in the late morning when prey animals may be hot and unalert. If it is not successful, the leopard may continue to hunt all afternoon.

► A leopard rests on warm sandstone rocks in Namibia.

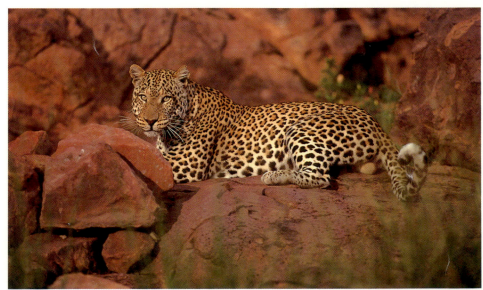

Threats

The adult leopard does not have any natural predators, although lions, hyenas, jackals and eagles will kill its cubs. The leopard is also threatened by other carnivores stealing its prey. Usually, when a leopard kills an animal that is not too heavy, it will drag the carcass up a tree.

Sometimes the animal is too heavy to do this, or there may not be a suitable tree available. If the leopard is not quick enough, lions or hyena will smell the carcass and arrive on the spot in minutes. They will drive the leopard away and steal its kill.

▼ These spotted hyenas have stolen a leopard's prey.

▲ A male lion walks past gazelle, a favourite prey animal of both lions and leopards.

The leopard also competes with other big cats such as lions and tigers for prey. But in Africa, since it has such a varied diet, the leopard doesn't often starve. The leopard's biggest threat is people.

Loss of habitat

Since the nineteenth century, when Europeans began to settle in Africa, many thousands of leopards have been killed due to shooting and loss of their home ranges to farming. When fences were put up around new farms, the habitat of both leopards and their prey was taken away.

When leopards started taking farm animals instead, farmers shot the leopards or laid out poisoned meat to kill them and protect their calves. Today, in many countries in Africa, the only leopards left are in national parks, where they can be protected.

LEOPARD LIFE SPAN

On average, leopards live up to twelve years in the wild and up to twenty years in captivity.

▼ This village of farms in Kenya is also the leopard's habitat.

► A beach vendor tries to sell a leopard skin in Sierra Leone, West Africa.

Skins

For many years leopard skins have been prized as fashionable coats and hats. In the 1960s, as many as 50,000 leopard skins were sold every year around the world. The leopard populations in Kenya, Ethiopia, Namibia and Zimbabwe were reduced by 90 per cent during the 1970s.

▲ These leopard, crocodile and snake skins were smuggled into Germany, where they were confiscated.

Today, the trade in leopard skins has been stopped in most of southern Africa and is now rare in parts of West and North Africa, India and Asia. The Convention on International Trade in Endangered Species (CITES) banned the sale of leopard skins in July 1975.

However, poaching and illegal trade continues. As long as people want to buy products made from leopards, there will always be poachers. To make matters worse, hunting for sport is still allowed. Wealthy people from Europe and America pay a fee to be able to shoot a leopard. It is only by understanding leopards and the threats they face that we might be able to stop them disappearing forever.

POACHING

On 20 December 1999, fifty leopard skins were seized in Ghazrabad, near Delhi.

●

On 12 January 2000, seventy leopard skins and 18,000 leopard claws were seized at Khaga, Utta Pradesh, in India. Other seizures in 2000 totalled 130 leopard skins and several thousand claws and bones.

▶ A poacher with a dead leopard in the Central African Republic. The sale of a leopard skin is an easy way to make money, but it doesn't help the poacher's country.

Leopard Life Cycle

 1 Newborn cubs are blind at first. Their eyes open when they are seven to ten days old. They grow fast on their mother's milk.

 2 When they are about two months old the cubs taste their first meat, which their mother tears from a carcass for them. Their mother's milk begins to reduce and they are weaned when they are about three months old.

 3 After the cubs are a year old, the mother may take them out on a hunting trip. She teaches them to be patient, stealthy and how to use their camouflage.

4 Before they are three years old, the cubs leave their mother to find territories of their own. The females may share part of their mother's range for a time but they have to keep away from her.

5 At three years old the young leopards are fully grown and ready to mate. The males may be ready to mate, but they face competition from older, stronger males.

6 Leopards live an average of twelve years in the wild.

SCIENCE
- Woodland and grassland habitat.
- Classification: mammals.
- Adaptation to habitat: camouflage.
- Leopard's life cycle.
- Food chain and pollution.

ART
- Shape and movement.

ENGLISH AND LITERACY
- Meanings of names: scientific and common.
- Write a story about a day in the life of a leopard.
- Conservation debates.

Leopard Topic Web

ICT
- Look at conservation groups' websites.
- Send an email to the government expressing a point of view.

MATHS
- Leopard numbers.
- Height and weight comparisons.

GEOGRAPHY
- Mapwork: where leopards live.
- Forests and grasslands.
- Tourism: safaris.
- Food journeys.

Extension Activities

English
- Debate whether leopards should be kept in zoos.
- Find and list collective names for groups of animals, or terms for their young eg cub, calf, chick.

Art
- Make a riverside forest frieze, with leopards and other animals that share their habitat.

Geography
- Trace a world map from an atlas.
- Draw a leopard distribution map.

Maths
- Use the leopard's head as a model to develop work on symmetry.

Science
- Make a display showing the ways in which leopards are adapted to their habitat.

Glossary

Camouflage To blend in with the background to become hard to see.
Carnivore Any animal that eats the flesh of another animal.
Dappled Patches of different colours and shades.
Dilate Grow bigger.
Extinct No longer existing.
Freezing When describing the action of leopard, this means to stay absolutely still.
Gazelle A type of antelope with large eyes found in Africa and Asia.
Gland A cell or organ found in the body.
Habitat The natural home for an animal or plant.

On heat Ready to mate.
Predator An animal that kills another animal for food.
Prey An animal that is killed by another animal for food.
Range The area in which certain plants or animals live naturally.
Stalk To approach without being seen or heard.
Sub-species Groups within a species.
Territory The area that is defended and controlled by an animal.
Thickets Dense bushes or undergrowth.
Wean When a young animal stops drinking its mother's milk.

Further Information

Organizations to Contact

Care for the Wild International
1 Ashfolds, Horsham Road
Rusper, West Sussex RH12 4QX
www.careforthewild.com

David Shepherd
Conservation Foundation
PO Box 123, Godalming
Surrey GU8 4JS
www.dshepherd.org

WWF-UK, Panda House
Weyside Park, Godalming
Surrey GU7 1XR
www.wwf-uk.org

Websites

PBS Kids
www.pbs.org
Use the search engine to find out about leopards and other wild animals, including video clips of a leopard stalking its prey.

The Discovery Channel
www.discovery.com
Talk to a leopard expert, and use the search engine to find out about leopards and other big cats.

Books to Read

Cats of Africa by Anthony Hall-Martin (Smithsonian Institution Press, 1998)

The Leopard Son: A True Story by Jacqueline Ball (McGraw Hill, 1996)

Natural World: Lion by Bill Jordan (Hodder Wayland, 1999)

Natural World: Tiger by Valmik Thapar (Hodder Wayland, 1999)

Index

Page numbers in **bold** refer to photographs or illustrations.